Triggers and Love

Poetry by
Aaron Joshua Perra

Potter's Wheel Publishing House
Minneapolis

Triggers and Love by Aaron Joshua Perra
Published by POTTER'S WHEEL PUBLISHING HOUSE
MINNEAPOLIS
MN 55378
www.POTTERSWHEELPUBLISHING.com

For permissions contact:
info@POTTERSWHEELPUBLISHING.com

ISBN: 978-1-950399-18-5
ISBN: 978-1-950399-19-2 (eBook)
LCCN: 2023942949

To Danny, Cheryl,
and to the suffering addict

Acknowledgement

First, I extend my heart to everyone still struggling with addiction. I also wish to express my gratitude to all those whom I have encountered along this journey, as well as all of the "normies" in my life.

To all my roommates in sober living who walk the same path as me. Your companionship and shared experiences have been invaluable on this road to healing.

To my sponsor who has taught me to let go of all the baggage I have been carrying on my shoulders, and to shine and be my true authentic self.

I am deeply thankful to my family who has stuck by my side through thick and thin. Their unconditional love and support have been a beacon of hope and strength for me. My mother who only ever wanted the best of the best for me, and my father who has constantly loved me.

To my lovers who have given me plenty of ammunition to write about.

Surprisingly, I want to thank my addiction. Amidst the struggles, I have discovered an inner strength that I had never known before.

Each day, I commit myself to stay vigilant against my addiction, and I embrace the learning and growth that accompany my daily experiences.

Throughout my progress, I recognize the guidance of my higher power, which has directed me in making crucial decisions along this path of recovery.

My heartfelt gratitude goes out to all those who have been a part of this transformative journey with me.

Contents

Forward

In the depths of agony and pain, where the darkness threatened to consume him whole, Aaron Joshua Perra found solace in the power of his own words. Trapped in the clutches of addiction, he fought a relentless battle, as his soul withered and his spirit faltered. But through it all, his pen became his weapon, his journal his sanctuary, and his poetry his saving grace.

Triggers and Love is a collection of journal entries that unveils the raw, unfiltered journey of a man struggling with addiction, heartache, and the pursuit of love. Aaron Joshua bares his soul with courageous honesty, allowing the reader to witness the darkness that once enveloped him, while simultaneously kindling a glimmer of hope within their own hearts.

The pages of this book breathe life into the shadows, illuminating the path towards redemption and healing. Aaron Joshua's words capture the essence of forbidden love and the desperation of addiction, ultimately guiding us towards the light that still flickers amidst the darkest nights.

As a witness to his journey, I have marveled at Aaron Joshua's resilience and unwavering commitment to his art. In the midst of his own turmoil, he has consistently found truth and solace through the brutal and beautiful honesty of his poetry. Triggers and Love is a testament to his indomitable spirit, a testament to the strength he has cultivated in the face of adversity.

Through his verses, Aaron Joshua aims to inspire others, to offer a lifeline of hope to those grappling with their own demons. His words are a reminder that even in the midst of despair, there is always a way out, a way to reclaim one's own light. This book is a beacon of hope, a reminder that no matter how deep the darkness may seem, there is always the possibility of finding solace and love.

I am honored to present Triggers and Love to the world, for within its pages lies a profound journey of self-discovery and resilience. Aaron Joshua's light has always found a way to shine through, and it is through his words that we, too, can find our own flicker of hope.

Cheryl Perterson

Journal Entries

Poem 1

January 6th, 2019

Egotistical manifestation
Failure to grow as a pubescent adult
Failure to be failed and sad
You knew how much I loved
You walked and never stopped
You couldn't let go of the animosity,
you didn't want to take the crown of constant longevity—
You chose the vowel that didn't start with hope
You pointed your tongue before your consciousness
You had to blind us with your alcohol
I had to distract us with abuse and confusion—
Pain, shame, guilt—
shadows that will forever be haunted by the momentum of my
unwillingness to give up
You looked at me with sickness and disgust but you only had to
look at your own reflection
I've fallen out of nothing that feels like everything
I've sacrificed so much for you, more for you than you will ever
have You hide behind your wall of liquids—
I've seen the unnecessary chaos you love to subliminally cause
I've felt the annihilation of your twisted consumption of
assumptions— It led all to insanity
It led to the sensational feeling of corruption and dementors I
hope the sun learns to shine freely without judgment
I hope the sky stays blue and bright
I hope you some day find the light.

Poem 2

January 31st, 2019

Learning how to walk in slow motion

Always getting caught up
In all the commotion

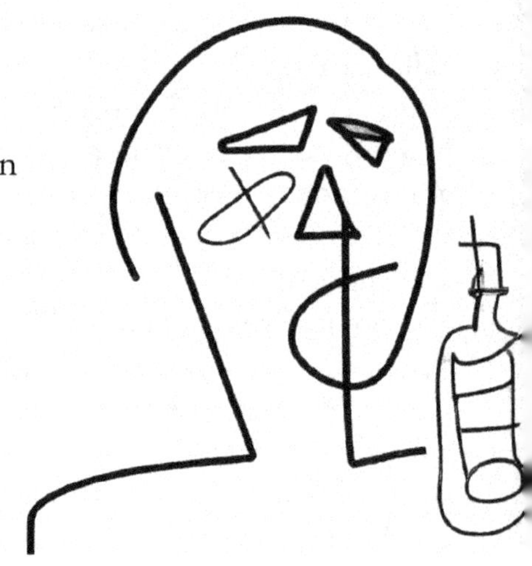

Imagining dipping my toes
Into the ocean,

If only there were a magic potion

My heart dedicated,
And filled with devotion.

Moving fast as a locomotive—
In constant motion.

Contamination lingering,
Distorting my imagination
Into a tangible creation.

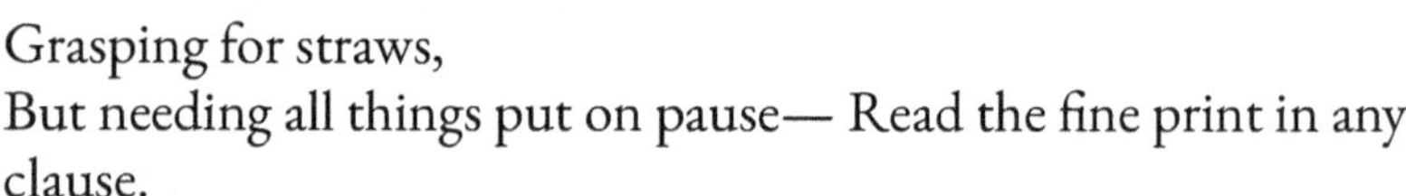

Grasping for straws,
But needing all things put on pause— Read the fine print in any clause.

Evidential corrosion,
Bodies wrapped and covered in gauze

The unwanted surrounding,
Clapping,
Giving applause—
Look at what all of you have caused.

Poem 3

July 27th, 2019

Unbeatable, beating summer—

I love you, sun—
How I adore you my little bumble bee. Look at all of your beauty.

You are so ever beautiful to me— The subtle fragrances, the wind carrying You throughout the gleaming world.

Everyone enjoying your presence, It's finally all about you.
It's always been about you.

From the first day, to the next,
You bring joy, comfort, and
Charisma.

You are what beauty will always Be.

Poem 4
August 23rd, 2019

Do you see the beaming joy you bring me?
Do you see the contentment—
The words I spoke to you, it will always be what I said and meant

Out of shape, and bent—
my heart collided in torment

My miraculous, magicianaly magical—
Always making sure you
Don't hear,
Just all the words I speak

I grieve, I cry,
Every single night....
I wish you were my.. my.. mine

It's a tremendous cruel crime—
My heart
will always be yours

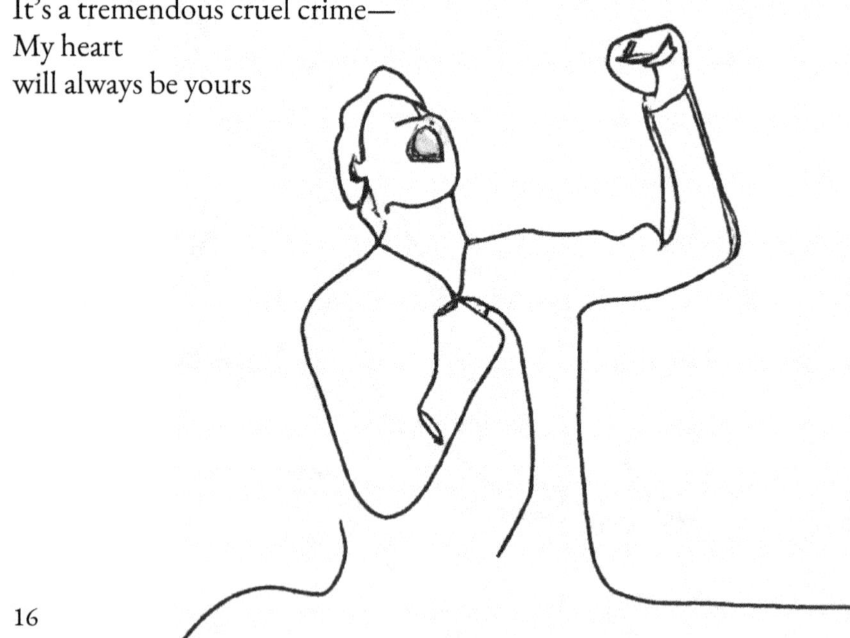

Poem 5

September 1st, 2019

I clearly see, there's no fit for me,
Tides shifting, heartstrings left un-tugged, contemplating the existence of me— Drifting away, to the sea.

Hindering thoughts of the unknown, my scope broken, the larger picture in life— blinded by my encumbering eyes.

Don't you see, it's clear to me, I see that there's just no fit for me— *Breathe, breathe, breathe—*
Just breathe.

Lost in translation, misunderstood—
No one is listening, everyone's full of responses—
with their eyes lacking in intelligence.

The cool air tickling at my bare feet, the quiet whispers from the wind, calming my restless mind—
Thank you Mother Nature for your undeniable companionship.

So unclear to see—
What will my future be,
Where will I find my fit—
And present all of ME.

Poem 6

September 1st, 2019

Harmonic happenings—
delicate illusions,
And the finest cuisine
silky lips, your sunset cheeks—
An undeniable
smile

Dialing back my cravings,
submerging my feels,
locking out my emotions—
Swimming without a raft
drowning lungs—
full of air

Contemplating circumstance, unequivocal rotations—
Drowning in my own flesh
Why are you deciding I'm clear like plastic, invisible to your
naked eye— Unjust love, or is it just Love

Uncontainable, my heart dives onto the floor—
beating to the beat-less,
Less and less
Do you even see me anymore,
Don't you feel,
Feel me, at the depths of your
inner core

Poem 7

October 13th, 2019

Molecular, microscopic induction—
A safe haven for thy heart.

I'm drifting to the ends of the nothing,
Setting sail; rain drenched silky veils.

I am only a man who knows no bounds—
Wearing my customized crown.

Motivational thoughts conveniently spiral like a whirlpool—
Indescribable,
but adaptable to all chaos that you propel.

Don't dwell on what has happened—
sadness swells on all the loved worthy hearts.

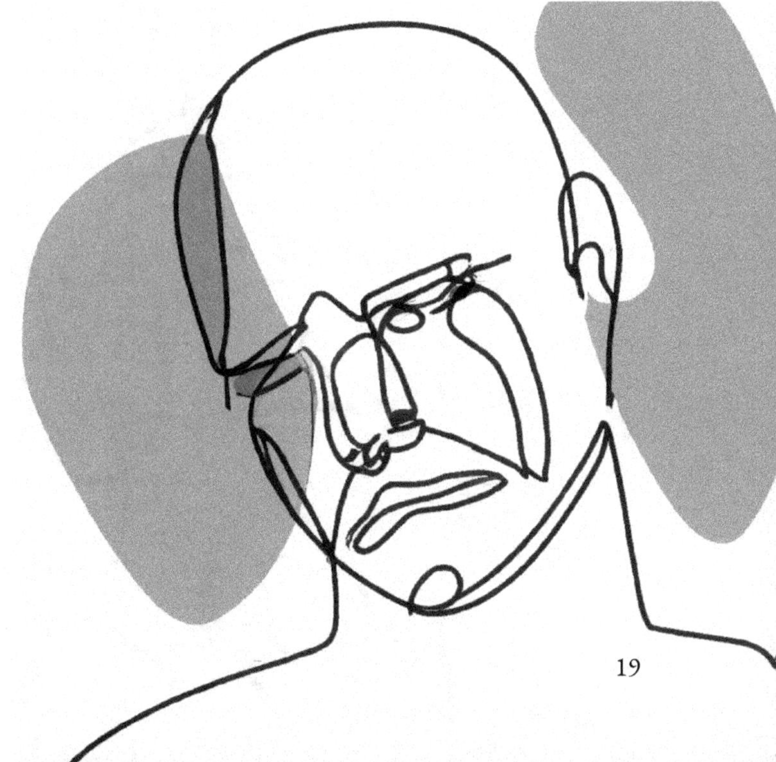

Poem 8

October 28th, 2019

A Divine moment—
Contemporary cosmic collisions—
A slither with my fervent tongue
Walk through my door,
and come over.

Feeling you, intertwining
skin touching—
Making velvet with every touch
On the floor making rituals.

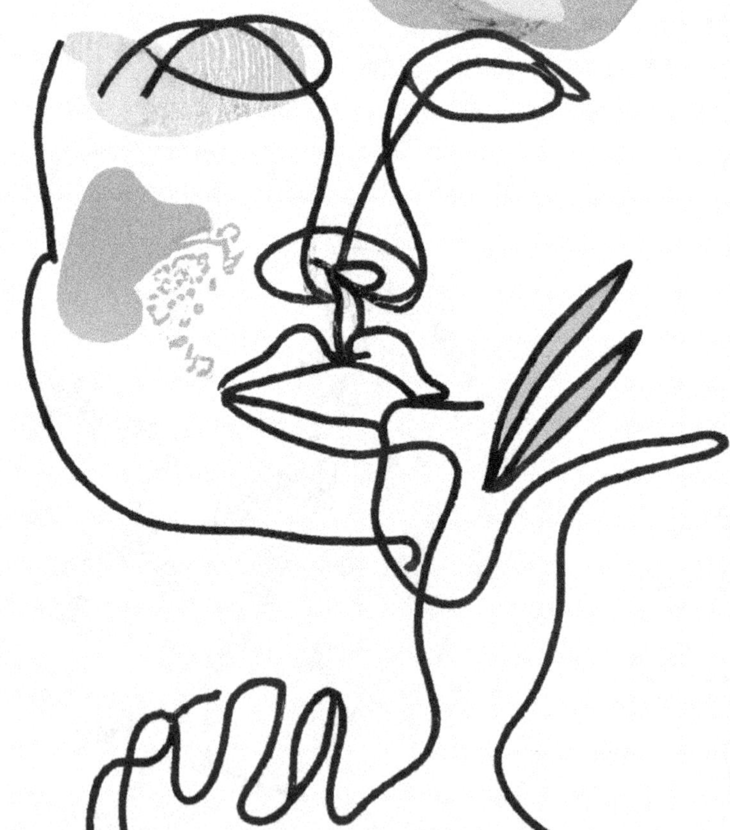

Poem 9

November 4th, 2019

Time passing by—

The illusion that heals all wounds

But then why does my heart ache

How to walk away, and take a break—
Wishing I were a simple snowflake
Or even frosting off a cake

Feeling fried and baked—

How much more spice and heat can I take My heart needs to take a break
Dodging all who are false and fake

Slivering and coiling—

ready to strike like a devilish snake

Only wanting to find the imperfect mate—
Things only happen when you stop chasing fate
It's time for my heart to take a break

Poem 10

November 15th, 2019

The day I die, is the only time I'll shine
When I die, is when you'll decide to be mine

Why blame me, when you were always my golden key

Why punish me, when you soberly flee,
Away from me

Could it be, you never really saw me, could it be, you were only full of your own delusional creed
The day I die is when I cry, saying goodbye to all the men who never took the title of being my bride

So many men full of pride, when eight days pass,
Remember how I died

Poem 11

November 16th, 2019

No more seasons to enjoy,
no more reasons to hold onto

Bitter hearts—
bodies crumbling apart

Feeling finite—
feeling bruised, broken, and abused

Running motionless—
So much energy at a loss
Beginning to become lost

Suffocating, squeezing life
Time slipping, watching the sand
Sifting slowly away

Gripping hair, strands falling
Tears dripping, showering myself in emotions

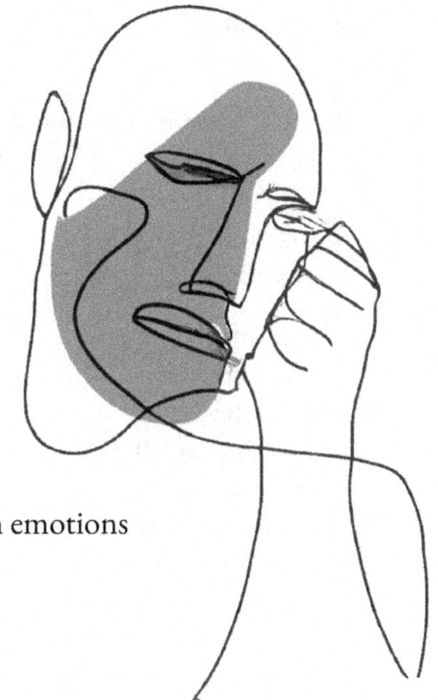

Poem 12

November 16th, 2019

I lay myself down to sleep,
Wanting this creeping of a feeling OFF!
and away from me—
Falling, falling,
into the deep

Scraping the inners of my brain, Finding me
in the center
Of it all—
Falling, falling,
Into the deep

Imogen Heap—
Just yet another
ambient daydream
Continuing to fall, fall,
Down, Into the deep
And now I lay myself down
to sleep

Poem 13

November 29th, 2019

I don’t care today,
Or tomorrow
I won’t even bother,
with the next day—
Either

Gluttony and punishment Is what to prevent,
But misery and company Are calling for crumpets, And tea

Flee, flee... Run away,
and dive into your
Damn, manifested pity
It harshly fills you With
Contemporaneous glee

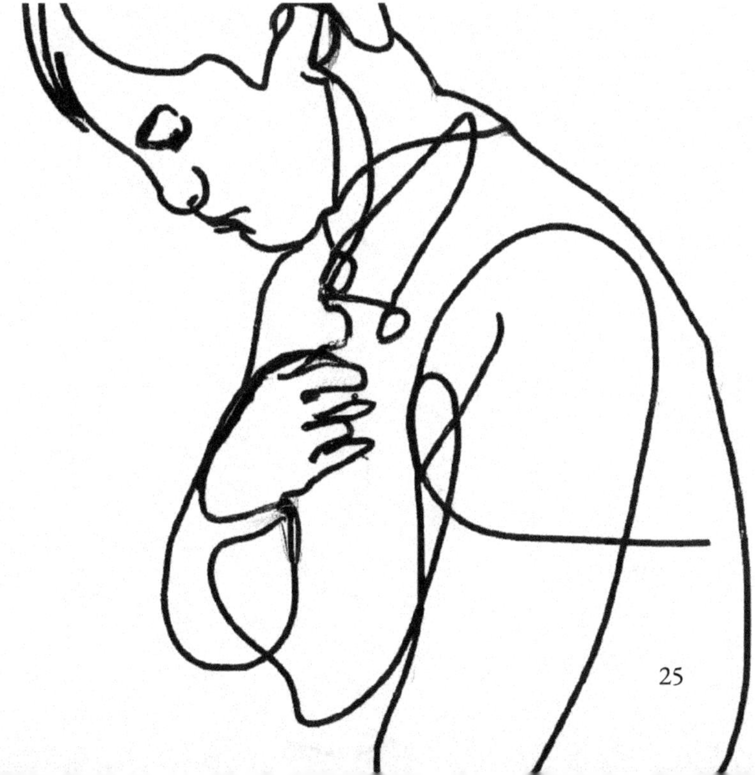

Poem 14

December 1st, 2019

Lost in love—

Isolation, continuation of the suffering
Fool

Modifications, solar beam manipulations,
God's creations

Reflection, conjunction, stuck on all my
Malfunctions

Contemplation, the thought to which I'm thinking of You

Causation, the crimson sings in sorrows, drifting away by The
silent Night

Poem 15

December 5th, 2019

So messed up, so delusional—
So messed up in it all, but don't you dare make the call

You were never apart of it all
You were lead to believe, and receive
You were just a thot, not even worth to be bought

You're not worthy of any type of price tag, your unholy looks make me choke and gag

Bring on your ugly, you just continue to remind me of the the word FUGLY

Poem 16

December 5th, 2019

Remembering when we first met There was so much excitement
our eyes content,
Smiles awkwardly bent

Before the night could end,
We learned how to sway and bend
We became undercover—
Secret lovers

Fixated on your true beauty—
Imagining the taste of your lips,
and then making my way
down, down,
caressing your silky skin, and hips

Remembering the day when
our eyes first met
Content with excitement
Nothing can compare
To the beauty
that is you

Asphyxiated with temptation
creating that intangible space,
Allowing myself to take in
your beauty and grace
I will not sever our entangled
heartstrings,
Like an ivory harp
bringing harmonic,
and savory dreams

Poem 17

December 5th, 2019

I'm losing the touch to life
The taste—
heaven's nectar
stranded, and feeling alone
The reality of it disappearing and gone
I frown upon you, and the drop of daylight's dew
It's always been about you—
Everything you are, you reflect my color, and it's so beautifully
and congruently bright-eyed
And oh, oh, oh, so blue
But I understand, it's not quite your
Hue

Poem 18
December 19th, 2019

I'm sorry for losing hope,
Hope in myself
I know you don't like me now, I know I pushed till there was no return
I'm sorry I am hurting,
Sorry for hurting you
Wanting to close every curtain
No more daylight in,
Collapsing from within.
Losing vision of that
Mysterious grin
Time for that date
With the devil
And a shot
of Gin.

Poem 19

December 28th, 2019

Just a constant thought of you,
never enough pictures could capture the continuation—
of this frustration.
Painting outside—
shading all trees, With their brushes,
admiring the beautiful leaves

They say it's okay to grieve,
I say continue to pour the mead—
Today I will please my greed
That sweet amber glaze—
From every wobbler's maze

Never wanted to say goodbye—
I know I'll see you around
You help keep my feet on the ground—
Hope you know we're bound
You and I are so very profound.

My feet weightless,
not one toe touching ground.

Poem 20

December 29th, 2019

Distortion, mega devastation,
A constant accumulation
Of my humiliation

Cataclysmic catastrophe—
A seismic shock,
A contingent block

I hear you talking smack,
Hearing you, but just barely—
No longer wanting you to get me

Forget me, don't envision me,
Don't waste time thinking of me—
You Lost your chance at knowing me

Shining and smiling with glee—
Yesterday, I took a stand for me
Today, I gain growth and personal fame
Worth the price, and no shame

To a degree, my memory plays tricks on me—
Just wanting you to please forgive me
All I know is I bleed for all of you
I just want to keep being everyone's glue

Always know my color and hue—
Any shade of blue will do,
Wishing you picked up on
All my subtle clues

Poem 21

January 4th, 2020

Just let me continue to drown
In misery and sorrow,
no more time to borrow

Let me just suffer—
The pity is too deep, and I am too weak I admit defeat
I'll soon be resting at your feet

I give up—
I just continue to get beat
Even when I beg and plead

Poem 22

February 10th, 2020

The bitterness of you all—
Consuming, floundering and flopping Drowning in my tear made puddles

Howling at the moon—
The lonely coyote sobs,
Waiting for it to return

The anguish and burn
Yet, the heart yearns—
The tapestry of you, is so irresistibly sublime

That perpetual blue wave—
My soul encased inside a cave,
The ocean clashing with my heart

I fell apart; never to escape,
My own revenge on oneself—
Caught in a cage, dreaming.

Poem 23

February 13th, 2020

When your words reflect hate

Creating misfortune and fate—

that you try to make!

Manipulating the frosting

into your perfect tasting cake

I'm bound to make that same mistake— And now the
consumption of erratic instant insanity— The calamity!
Baked and seared, escalating, and hesitating
Devastating devotion to all of your
locomotion

Continuing to cause unwanted commotion
Dropping the notion, drinking every last drop
From your irresistible potion

Poem 24

May 30th, 2020

Stuck in a place that
I cannot escape
A prisoner in the mainframe of my brain
Boxed up, and arranged,
an emotional crane—
Rummaging through the heart ache and pain
Dwelling in the depths of my insanity
In search of hope, but inside here,
I prefer to walk and pout, continue to gloat
Pulling at every blood vessel and vein hoping
for an electrical charge
to change.

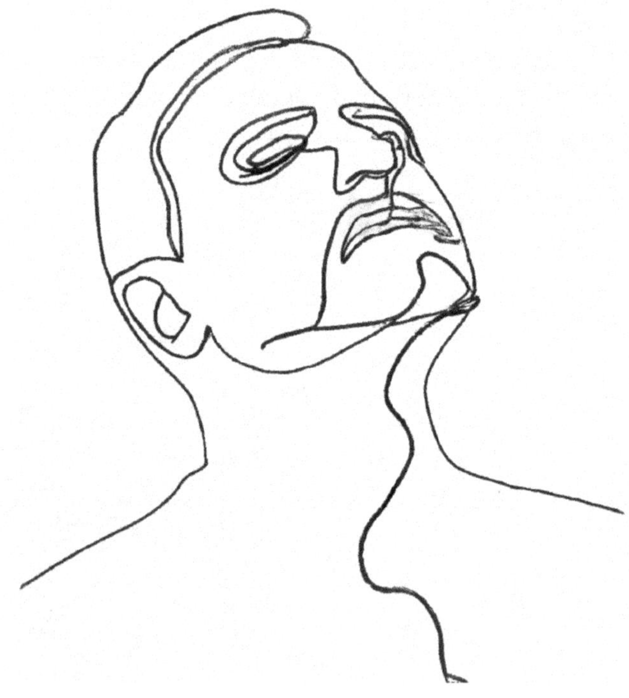

Poem 25

May 30th, 2020

Trying to let things be,
Trying to just wait and see,
Creating joy of my own
Always wanting a happy heart—
Someone's home
Nothing's wrong with wanting love,
If it's meant to be,
We will soon all see
Remembering to try to let things be,
To just try to wait and see.

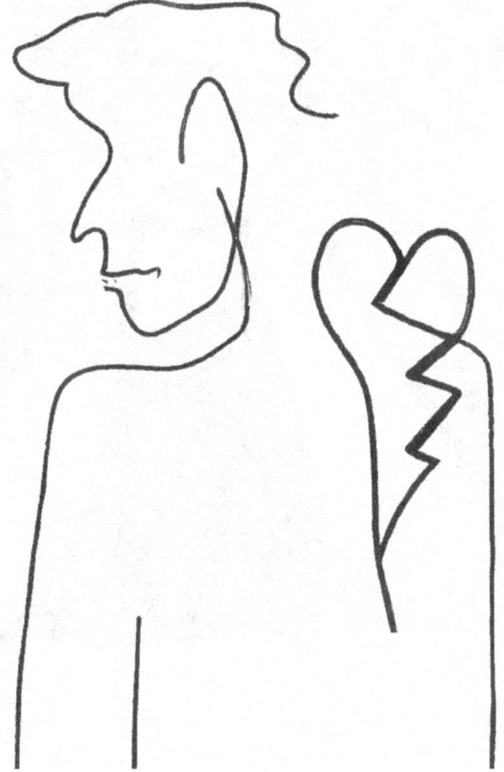

Poem 26

June 9th, 2020

I designate, to deliberate our squandering quarrels
How I hate to fight against my ethics and morals
Both fearful of what we cannot control
But remain hopeful
Even when the dark clouds loom

Poem 27

July 30th, 2020

How I miss you,
when I awake every morning,
The hurt bleeds into my unconscious.

Lately, sleep has been the only break
From heartache.

Recreate the most beautiful mistake,
We both knew eventually it would break.

How long will we have to go on,
Without one another around.

Every part of me becomes unbound— Unraveled.
I plead that someday you'll come back to me,
Just come home to ME.

Poem 28

August 30th, 2020

Over and over, a tormented circle—
Going round and round,
tethered and tied down to the ground.

Always feeling bound and chained to shame—
The humiliation game.

Restraint, Retract, Retreat—
Walk to the sound of a broken drum beat.
Hopeless and feeling defeated—
History repeated.

A fool has been created,
Feeling cheated, the world being mistreated—
Gone, wandering round and round—
Exhausted and depleted.

Poem 29

August 31st, 2020

Wandering through the willow of whispers
Distracted by the swarms of voices
Some making the most shrieking noises

Blinded by the complete darkness
How am I going to get out of this This feeling—
Swallowed
by the
Black abyss

HELL
sealing it with a kiss
And the devil taking a piss
Death is this—
Your body burned to a crisp.

Poem 30
September 2nd, 2020

I don’t know how to let it be
I wish I could be set free
But that will never be
Just listen to his decree

You are a forever nocturnal dream
A visual spectacle, I find you so exceptional
You are so irresistible, Your lips kissable So kissable, they are admissible

How is this possible
My heart, the bullseye to your crossbow
Floating on a cloud, dodging every pothole
You even have a sexy clavicle

Can we just lay together
And observe the weather
Your skin supple, soft as a feather
Admiring your brilliance, and at being clever

Trying to catch my breath
How you make my mind a mess
I digress,
you are impeccable, and delectable

Your body, so delicious
I’m ravenous and vicious for
your liberal kisses
Seduce me now,
with your midnight neck kisses

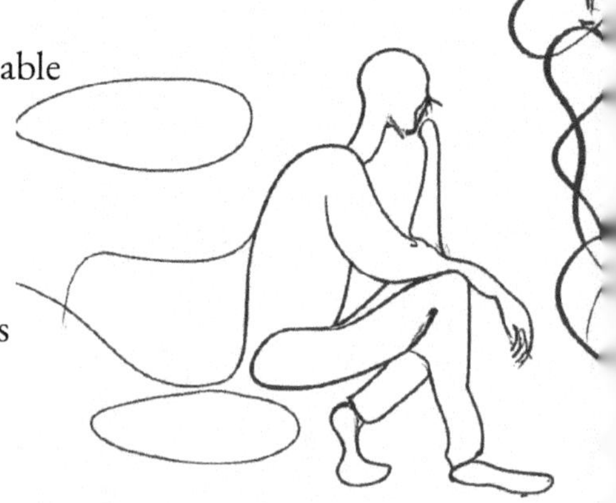

Poem 31

September 13th, 2020

I'm tired of being lonely and insufficiently amusing.
Solitude doesn't put me in the right mood— If anything,
it's gasoline
to my fire.

Buyer beware—
he hasn't been handled
with very much care;

Used and abused,
A glutton for punishment—
An eager beaver awarding himself with unpleasantness—
A constant, degrading pest

Visualize
these vultures connive,
Roosting from their nest—
Fumes of narcissism
emitting from their
Constant crowing

Only fragments of you exist,
So this is bliss,
heaven forbids another kiss
And I persist to
agree with them (on this)

Poem 32

October 2nd, 2020

I shed a tear and you don't care

We eat at each other's ankles like whorish hyenas

Taking turns with our battlecries

Why won't you hear me out for just one second

Bending time seems more tangible than the flesh around your pulsating heart

The corrupt landscape made by your hands
The denying of your own faults

I want to walk across all of the lands that are scattered throughout

I wanted you to be the land,
I am the ocean

You once trusted me,
I once had your trust

I trashed your heart with my foolishness
I peeled back the skin from your integrity

Devastation, devastated
Your revenge

My pain accumulating and ready to thunder and pour

The sun will continue to rise, the wind will still blow

If you listen, you will hear its call

Poem 33

October 4th, 2020

Goodbye sweet life—
Just how bitter I thought you were But now heading down,
straight down Everything—
ambiguous
curious
enigmatic, fanatic

Torpedoing through the turbulence—
A sublime brilliance encasing each memory—
Flashing before my eyes
Fragmented pieces—
Shattering with non-stop thoughts
Teasing with nakedness
Silky soft, like your kindness—
Sweeter than the morning dewdrops

Contemporary visuals and feels—
Imagining you in every light possible,
Every reel of film capturing every inch
Of your silhouette, all so well kept—
You have soul and depth

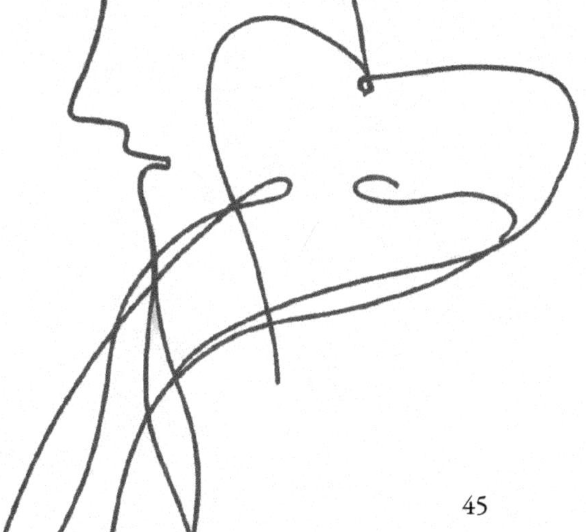

Poem 34

October 4th, 2020

Walking on the droplets from November's rain
The unknown makes a splash,
and takes its reign
Sometimes dripping with indifference
A preferable preference
Sadness has commenced
Dressed like the rest
Trying to beat the best
I digress, back to the embryo,
Back to the nest—
A baby's birth breaking crest
I always mean to be the best,
Unfortunately feeling like a pest—
Having a hard time trying to digest
Lost in all of this, and now failing, falling, floundering—
Come around again, reach around my waist, again I'm just
wanting to learn how to sway and bend with you—
Please let me be perpendicular with you—
Lying next to you makes me feel crystal blue,
your most beautiful hue.

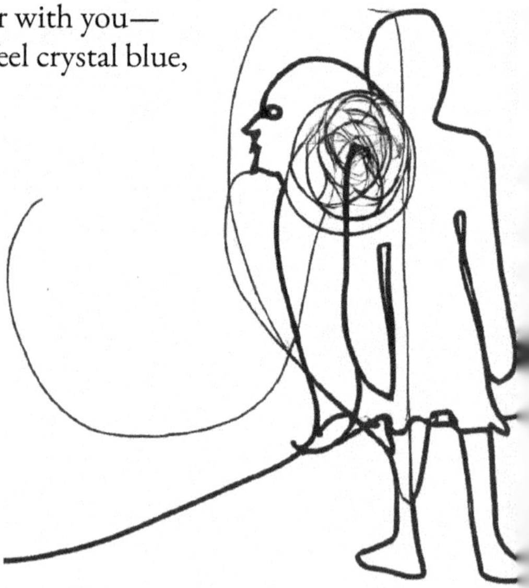

Poem 35
October 4th, 2020

Constantly reminded of the relationship that doesn't exist
How lovely to have a secret lover—
A lover that is non-existent, a mirage,
A figment of the other person's thoughts
Imagining the handlings of your touch—
Smooth and rough, seeing you in your beauty and buff
How I so wish you'd see all of me and not through me—
The vibes we feel are so very intense and real, like you're kind of a BIG deal—
Mesmerized by your charm and decadent feels

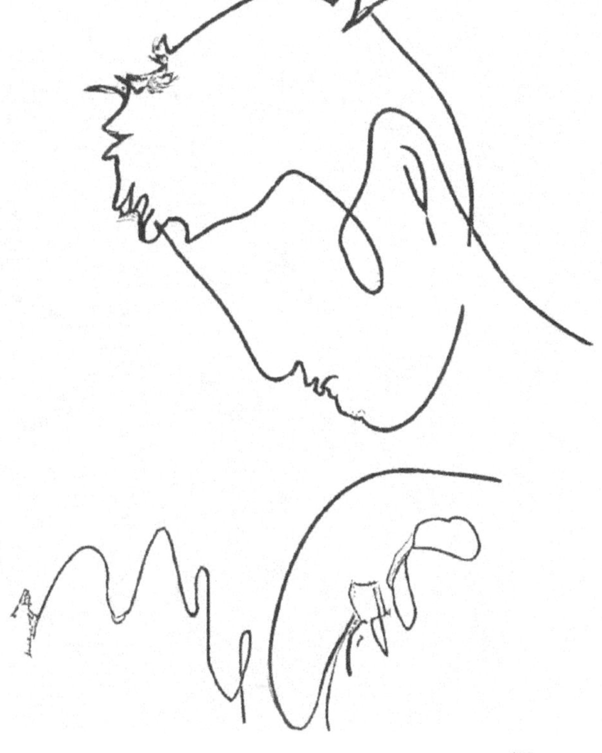

Poem 36

October 6th, 2020

I see you, and your brilliantly blue iridescent hue, Shining bright and beautiful,
Your kisses as fresh as the morning dew—
Your vibrancy cannot be compared to any other light
Your atmosphere, bringing me higher than a kite Dancing on my heels all through the night
Trickled with delight
Daydreaming about you, and your might

Poem 37

November 20th, 2020

You're like a shadow that never fades
You're that torturous fly
On the wall
You're the epitome
Of annoyance
You're selfishly
Narcissistic,
But you pretend
To be a friend
Wanting to kick it
You don't care
To bare
Who you are
You're a careless
Coward
You're a suffocating
Dilemma
I am drained
Exhausted
I am beat

Poem 38

November 24th, 2020

Always wishing
dreaming for that love
To imagine flying away
on the back of a dove

Living in the greenest of all coves Flowers springing up from the soil birds and butterflies coming back in droves Drifting in the bliss of happiness

Craving for just one more kiss
Is this what heaven is
If only I could experience this
Or will I forever be dancing in the mist

Contemplating my own existence
My heart hurting
From emptiness
Is this the true test

Of selflessness
Or sheer ignorance
Searching for love just leads
to carelessness
Even misery admires
company

Poem 39

December 1st, 2020

Escaping sleep, the mind on override—
vague chattering, hollow voices
Continuous haunting throughout the night

Trying to muster up some might
for the great fight
But rather, flee than fight
Fly away on an ambiguous kite

Contagious and bound tight
Torturous nightmares only after midnight
Can't breathe, my throat tight
Just once more, wanting to fly high like a kite

Waking up in the morning, or less—
And feeling the crimsons burning bite
Will I always feel affright
Take me away my friendly kite

Poem 40

December 21st, 2020

Running away, far away,
To only be sinking,
Sinking In quicksand

Dismembered, disbanded,
Body fragments have landed It's only what god commanded

Waiting, wishing on you,
To rush on down,
Bound, wearing your crown

Tranquil, ambient chaos
You're the finer things,
Seductive in your woven tapestry

Your body, a stunning masterpiece—
A soul seeking release
I can see your beautiful inner beast

How the thought of you
Is so bright blue
Your skin as soft as the morning dew

Poem 41

December 22nd, 2020

Sadness fluttering its wings
disguised in the beauty of a butterfly

Overwhelming disbeliefs
Every bucket filled with grief

Concrete sheets,
melting heart-beats
My soul drifting down vacant streets

Mirror imaging defeat
No longer feeling nice and neat Protect me from the flesh eating creep

Reminiscing the summer breeze
How it used to put me at ease
There's no way to please

Falling to the ground on my knees
I'm told otherwise,
but I disagree

Poem 42

January 21st, 2021

Looking for love
In the darkness

Searching for
That unmistakable bliss
Of a kiss

Instead,
I find
A serpent's hiss

Twisting down,
Interwoven—
In a cloak
Of dark mist

Squeezing my hands
Into
A tightly bound fist !

When will I
No longer be
Angry and pissed ?

Shrouded
In complete,
Utter darkness—
Get the gist ?

Poem 43

January 24th, 2021

Don't waste your grace
On the displaced
Refuting—
Nothing needs fine-tuning
But no matter,
You'll always be
Bothered and bewildered

Nothing is being hidden,
Or filtered
Just thoughts off kilter

Our friendship matters more,
It's like your favorite
Milky, warm sweater
It's softness
Always making things better

Remember that our friendship
Is the reflection of the most Beautiful weather
It will always make the darkest of days
Brighter and better

When in doubt,
Scrounge up and find
That milky, warm sweater
That always makes everything
Ever so better

Poem 44

April 6th, 2021

They think I'm a dart,
worn and broken, with a bent flight
But throughout the night,
Their bombs go off—
With such delight

My mind synchronizing just right,
With just enough levels of fear and fright
Keep feeding them their succulent, salacious, sweet bites—
Licking lips, mouthwatering, jaw dropping disaster

This brings happiness and pleasure to the darkest of demons,
to their ungrateful master
They prance around enjoying their own nauseating chatter—
Served to you on a silver platter.

Poem 45

April 18th, 2021

It's been quite sometime now,
Since you left,
and went away

Everyday, I imagine
waking up next to you,
But my imagination unreliably true

Standing still, but my thoughts
Of you,
Still traveling through

Stuck and tangled in a mindful maze Standing at the edge of a cliff,
creating mischief
Grazed thoughts of "forget me knots"

You are my weakness,
You are my crux,
You are my equinox

Poem 46

June 9th, 2021

A bucket with a hole,
Never full,
No sense of delight or fulfillment
Only to feel
Unwanted, used,
And bent

Left outside
To rust—
Kicked around,
A perfect bucket
To be discarded,
And tossed

Just an old bucket,
That has seen better days—
Tarnished, rusted
metal,
Once was whole
Without a hole

Poem 47
June 25th, 2021

Incongruent, melodic movements
Forced to make improvements
My soul, dead and dormant A delusional hermit
A recluse tiptoeing in the shadows
Lost in the depths
of my waterless shallows
The magnificent universe
I'm an unbroken curse
There's nothing else
To rehearse.

Poem 48

June 29th, 2021

You make my heart beat in more than one way
You make it ricochet
Let me be your window display
Watch me dazzle, dance, and play

Cerulean blue, Cupid's cue
How I want my hands
All over you

How dare you know
That I want more
How it eats at my core
Continuous jaw dropping to the floor

Destined—
Jepson blue, I love you

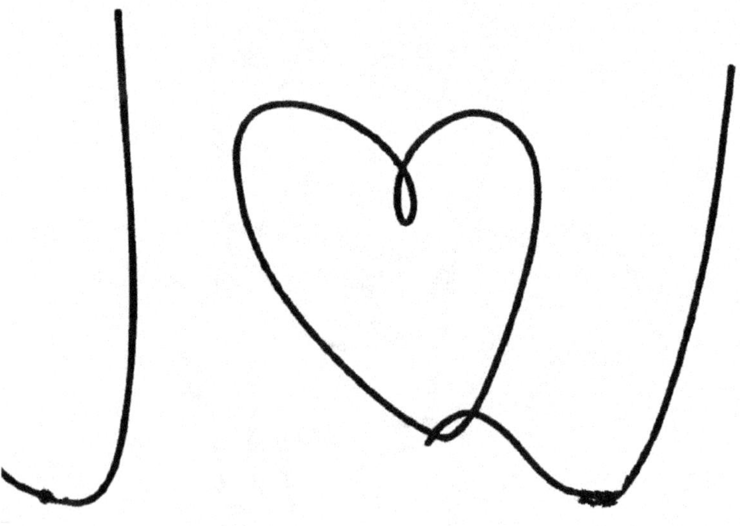

Poem 49
August 1st, 2021

I beat myself up,
And,
It's no secret—

No exit strategy,
My head
down shaking—
Feeling
your disbelief—
Pain and grief

Now, relief.

Poem 50

November 18h, 2021

Gouging Holes; actual negative space,
Missing flesh,
from a tongue—
And no stranger to me

Swollen, grinding, literal poison
extinguishing any joy, and happiness
A consistent cycle—
of missing Opportunity knocking

An epiphany triumphantly swimming,
Upstream—
Realizations lighting up the most brilliant of Christmas lights

Childish, immature—
Mentally, subconsciously, stunted growth.
inadequately psychosocially—
But a disadvantage is hard to admit

The black, dark, pit—
The gravity pulling all your hopes away
Just in time for rot, and decay
Continue to pay the crypt keepers way

Poem 51

December 7th, 2021

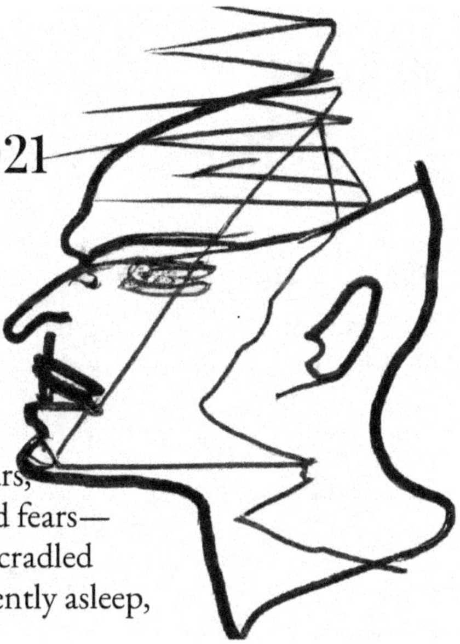

Never have I ever been so torn
Pent up, built up, emotions—
Rubber binders snapping,
On already broken skin

Setting sail, brushing off my tears,
Mirrors reflecting the unwanted fears—
Bare, and naked, wishing to be cradled
Wanting to be held, drifting silently asleep,
with the weight of my tears—
my eyelids so undeniably heavy

That familiar emotion causing all of the commotion
Engulfed by the ocean, with mist and salt
My soul, doesn't want you to go
But then go, just leave—
The upheaved, the torment of time

The words you'll say when you speak,
The quiet consuming the moment,
The gentle phase of goodbyes—
See how a baby infant cries

It's December, and still trying to mend myself
From being torn,
I can remember every moment that was made for you and I
And I Cannot deny the constant dreams of you
Always. Just. There.

Poem 52

December 12, 2021

It's bright and blue,
Yet, it's been fate tolerating hate,
Hellfire burning at your heels,
How to deliberate—
Politically tolerable,
like bleach, and hollow's

Create dismay—
Clay, molded, monument-al
the most seldom days
It's a haze,
It's been quite the day

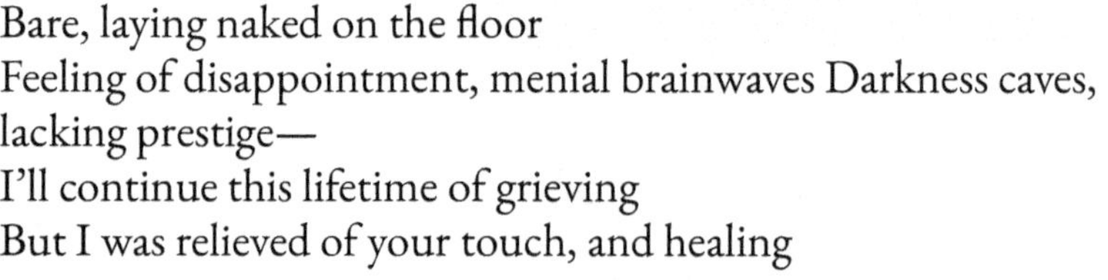

Bare, laying naked on the floor
Feeling of disappointment, menial brainwaves Darkness caves,
lacking prestige—
I'll continue this lifetime of grieving
But I was relieved of your touch, and healing

My blood, red, purple, and a hue of hope I am internally
bleeding—
Hamptons, cramped spaces,
these are All of those FBI cases
My brain in a perpetual circle, and all those hurdles

Every substance of food, digesting in my stomach—
Curdles
Harry Potter? Yea, Myrtle still cries
And at my Demise—
I carry & sail with all low's, and high's, wailing cries

Poem 53

December 30th, 2021

Those moments,
Those precise moments where you evolve You feel the air, and elevation beneath,
Beneath The soles of your feet

The heart, beating and fleeting, surreptitiously
Filled with joy, and discretion
Did I mention,
The suspense, and omission

I wish every thought was special,
And glistened, this was once my mission,
To give a thoughtful deposition,
And bring things to fruition

Wait, I forgot my dictation,
Can you hear the distinction?
Did I mention those moments,
those precise moments
Is it,
is it everything you'd think it would be

Do you finally feel free?
Do you see me?
I'm Smiling,
smiling back at you with glee
Remember, remember This,
this is me

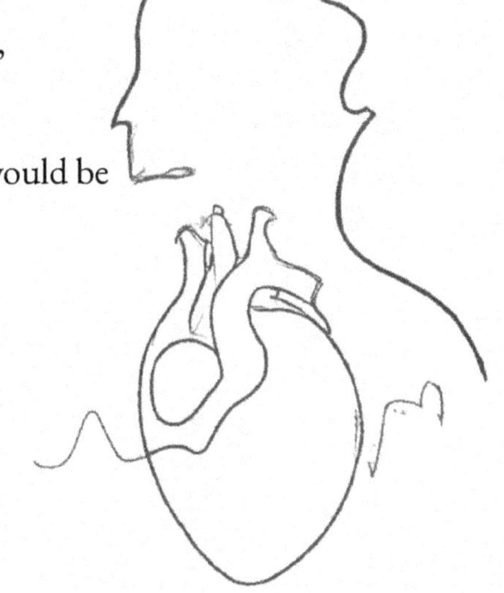

Poem 54

July 7th, 2022

I lay lonely in my bed
Wondering what may have been said
The echoing silent chatter—
ruminating matter, contingent clatter
Negative space encapsulates
Degrading, grinding gears
Their clanking anomalies
How I've fallen, hitting the ground with my knees
Debris, and a blood shed bed
Weeping willows, billowing on Earth's pillows
Insides of me constantly quivering,
Continuous questioning
The constant mentioning
The summoning; the queen
I will die, and they will spit on my grave
Asking me to behave
You're a cave,
You're a cove of the most forgotten individual
Hand them a knife
Playing tic-tac-toe on my jugular

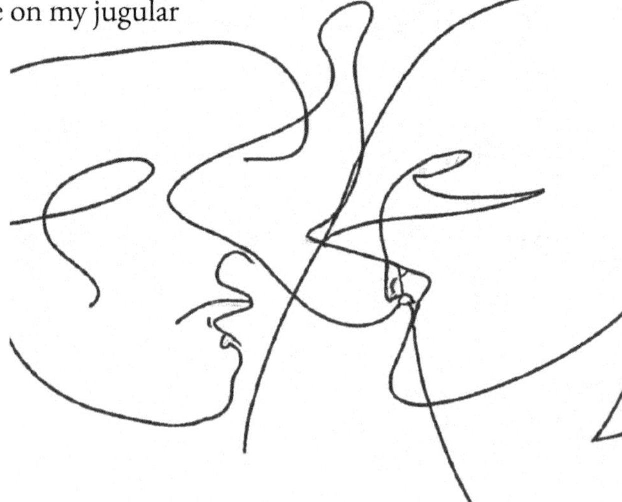

Poem 55

November 14th, 2022

Dear Tina,
It was love at first taste—
My first time kissing clouds
How others involved, blew it in my face
Not even knowing that behind the curtains, I was falling from grace.
I wish I had busted out the mace,
and sprayed it in your face.
I was only twenty-one,
But now with impending doom and gloom—
If I had only known better.
How you remind me of all the mischievous Heathers, you are so quite clever—
You caught me when I was the most vulnerable,
But I made the choice to make you my most, my one and only—
I ended up becoming so goddamn lonely,
and now I'm stuck in the "If Onlys".
But you told me you still loved me and would coddle, and hold me.
With my heart hurting,
and slowly hardening—
Becoming stone, like hollow bones, becoming brittle and broken—
I'm not even worth one golden token.
You are arbitrary—
You are a dumb ass fast, that didn't last,
You threw out a line, you casted your trap, and I fell for your hook,
You are a goddamn crook!
You took all of me—
You are full of greed, and I made you a need.

You became something that I couldn't live without, you normalized my use, And your abuse.
You caused a disorder—
Talk about a natural born murderer.
Clever, clever, clever—
Say goodbye to all of my endeavors,
But I am done, done with you robbing my joy.
Aaron Joshua 2.0 is ready, and deployed—
The courage is coming out,
And I'm going to win,
Win this match,
There is no catch,
I'm knocking you out, you're out.

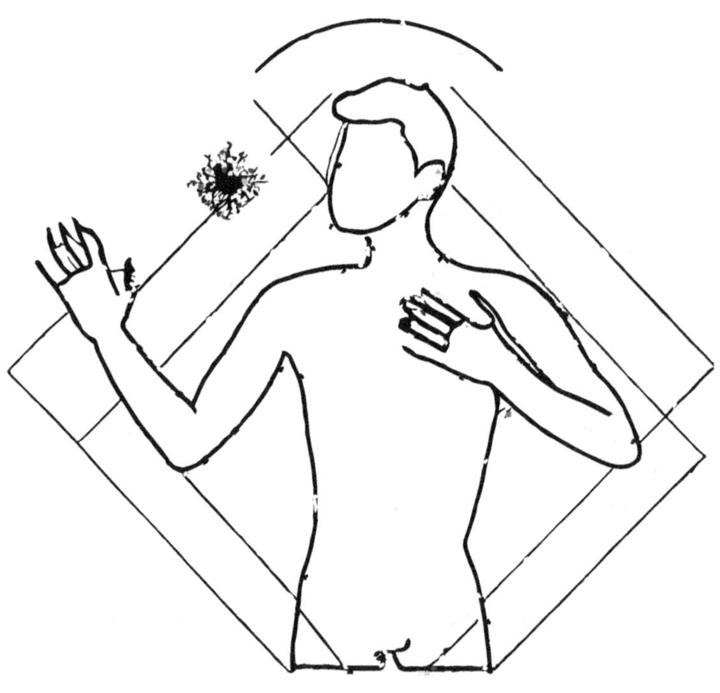

www.ingramcontent.com/pod-product-compliance
Lightning Source LLC
LaVergne TN
LVHW010107110826
845155LV00028B/533